Charlie and Elly Stories

Charlie and Elly Stories

FRANCES FARRER

Illustrated by Susie Jenkin-Pearce

LONDON
VICTOR GOLLANCZ LTD
1987

First published in Great Britain 1987
by Victor Gollancz Ltd,
14 Henrietta Street, London WC2E 8QJ

British Library Cataloguing in Publication Data
Farrer, Frances
  Charlie and Elly stories.
  I. Title   II. Jenkin-Pearce, Susie
  823'.914[J]   PZ7
  ISBN 0-575-03966-3

With love to everyone who helped,

especially M. R.

Photoset in Great Britain by
Rowland Phototypesetting Ltd, Bury St Edmunds, Suffolk
and printed by St Edmundsbury Press Ltd,
Bury St Edmunds, Suffolk

Contents

Charlie and Elly and the Snow

In January it snowed a lot. It snowed on the roofs and the chimney pots and on the lamp-posts and the cars, and in the gardens and all over the walls and gates— and it snowed so much on the road and the pavement that you almost couldn't tell which was which, or where the step down was from the pavement to the road.

Charlie and Elly and Robin the dog liked all this very much indeed. They made a slide on the ice in their garden and they played snowballing and making snowmen, and they took crusts out to feed the birds. Charlie was good at sliding and he threw snowballs very straight. When he wanted to hit something he usually did. Lots of people were amazed at how good Charlie was at throwing, because Charlie was just four. But he was good at all sorts of things like that, and balancing, and climbing trees.

One morning when Charlie and Elly woke up they heard a funny noise outside. It was quite a regular noise and it went *scrape-scrape-splat*, and sometimes *scrape-splat, scrape-splat*. Elly got up and ran to the window. Elly was almost five, and she always liked to know everything that was going on.

"Look, Charlie!" she shouted. "It's Jackson and Sailor. They've got spades and they're digging. They're digging the snow all up!"

"What for?" asked Charlie.

"Don't know," said Elly, "let's go and ask them."

So they got up as quick as they could. You never knew what Sailor and Jackson might be up to. They *did* have adventures. Sailor was Jackson's uncle but he didn't come home all that often because he was mostly at sea, travelling the world, thinking and looking, and carving flutes and whistles from bits of wood. Sailor was a brilliant carpenter and he could make practically anything out of wood. He was odd and very magic, and he got on really well with Jackson. They did things together without saying very much, just getting on.

By the time Charlie and Elly were dressed the scraping noise had stopped, but they went outside anyway. Mum had helped them to put on their big jumpers and their coats and hats and boots and gloves and scarves. Robin went outside with them. He didn't have to put anything on at all.

Sailor and Jackson were leaning on their spades gazing at nothing. Jackson always wore clothes with holes in and patches, and he did his hair so it stuck straight up in spikes, as if he'd had a shock. He always looked funny, but somehow he looked even funnier in the snow.

The snow had all disappeared from Miss Myrtle's front path, and from Charlie and Elly's. Elly marched up to them.

"What have you done with our snow?" she said, rather crossly.

"Hello kids," said Jackson, "what's the matter, eh? We cleared the snow and we done a good job! Look! It's really good, that is . . . We're freezin' now," he added.

"We shovelled the snow away so Miss Myrtle wouldn't slip and maybe fall down," said Sailor. He was often better at explaining things than Jackson was.

"I like snow," said Charlie, "why did you do our path?"

"Don't want you two falling down, do we?" said Jackson.

"We wouldn't!" said Charlie and Elly together.

"Robin might," suggested Sailor, who liked to keep the peace.

Just then Mr Patel from the corner shop came down the street.

"What a wonderful job you've done, Mr Sailor. And Jackson," he said. Mr Patel was a bit nervous of Jackson because of his clothes and spiky hair, so he talked to Sailor again.

"Please will you clear the path outside my shop?" he asked. "I can't do it myself because the shop is already open and I can't leave my customers. But I don't want them to slip and fall down in the snow."

"Ah no, we're freezin'," said Jackson, "Charlie and Elly's was going to be the last. We've had enough."

Sailor, though he wouldn't have said it quite like that, made a face to show he agreed.

"I'm very sorry you're tired," said Mr Patel, "but I must say please once again. It's extremely icy outside my shop."

"All right," said Sailor, giving in, "but you really are the last."

So they all marched off to Mr Patel's, the two snow clearers, the two children, and Robin.

At last Charlie and Elly found out about the noise that had got them out of bed. The *scrape* sound was the spade sliding under the snow and the *splat* was when the snow was thrown to the side of the path. Jackson and Sailor went on clearing. After they'd watched for a minute, Charlie and Elly started throwing snowballs, and Robin ran a bit further away, because Charlie's aim was excellent.

Just when Mr Patel's path was nearly finished, Mrs Rotten came out of her house, complaining as usual. Mrs Rotten was Charlie and Elly's neighbour but one, next door to Miss Myrtle. No-one could remember any more what her real name was, she had been called Mrs Rotten for such a long time. She was usually cross about something, that's why.

"What an awful noise!" she said, "that noise woke me up, it sets your teeth on edge, I think it's terrible on such a nice quiet morning. Who is it? Might have known *he'd* have something to do with it," she finished, pointing at Jackson. But then she saw that the paths were clear. Suddenly it looked like a good idea.

"On the other hand, you could do mine," she said.

"NO!" said Sailor and Jackson together, Sailor very softly and Jackson very loud.

"You must be bloomin' jokin', Mrs," Jackson went on, by way of explanation.

"Oh go on, you've done all the others, you must be in the swing of it now," said Mrs Rotten very plaintively. She still thought she might persuade them.

"Charlie and Elly's was to have been the last, but then Mr Patel's really was the last," said Sailor firmly. "We're tired now."

Mrs Rotten changed her tune immediately and became the cross Mrs Rotten that everybody knew so well.

"Pair of layabouts!" she shouted, "work-shy, that's

your trouble! Clear three paths, that's a day's work to you." Then she yelled straight into Jackson's face, "When I was fourteen I knew what work meant! And I didn't cheek my elders and I didn't tear holes in good clothes my parents had sweated to get me and I didn't stick my hair to look like a hedgehog and I didn't . . ." But we shall never know what else Mrs Rotten didn't do when she was fourteen, because Elly couldn't stand it any longer and she spoke up bravely.

"Jackson's nice, I like him," she said. Elly always stuck up for people she liked. And at that moment two more things happened: one of Charlie's biggest and best snowballs hit Mrs Rotten full on her leg, and Robin ran across Mrs Rotten's snowy path.

"YOU KIDS!" screamed Mrs Rotten as loud as could be. She was beside herself with anger. "My goodness, I'll speak to your mother . . ." and she went on screeching for what seemed like ages. Charlie and Elly were a bit scared, even though they thought it was funny too, but for Sailor and Jackson it was almost impossible not to laugh. Robin ran off round the corner because he hated rows, and as usual it was Sailor who thought of something helpful to say.

"I think the snowball was meant for Robin, I'm sorry it missed," he suggested calmly. Everybody knew it wasn't, but still it was a clever thing to say.

"Shouldn't be throwing them in the street anyway," Mrs Rotten sputtered on, but she wasn't as loud as before. Then she thought of something.

"You'd better make it up to me by doing my path!"

she said triumphantly. And Sailor had to come to the rescue once again.

"Where's Robin?" he asked in a loud and worried voice. "We'd better go and look for him!" And they all went off as fast as they could, shouting "ROBIN!" at the tops of their voices.

Robin was quite busy round the corner, sniffing in people's dustbins. He came rushing up, slipping and slithering all over the pavement. Then everybody started to throw snowballs, and you could easily see that Sailor and Jackson had forgotten what it was to be tired and cold, and that Charlie's aim was truly brilliant. Playing with the snow was more fun than clearing it, by a very long way.

Miss Myrtle and the Toyshop

Generally speaking, January is a rotten month for a birthday. It was Elly's bad luck that hers was at the beginning of January when it was usually snowing or cold, when people were feeling a bit flat after Christmas, and said they were sorry they couldn't get her a bigger present but they were still broke from buying Christmas presents.

Miss Myrtle understood all this very well, and when Elly's birthday came round she thought of a plan to make it very special indeed. She told Mum the plan, and Mum thought it was excellent.

"Charlie and Elly," said Mum, the day before the birthday, "you know what, Miss Myrtle's got a super treat for both of you tomorrow. She's going to take you to the biggest toyshop in town and find a present for Elly's birthday, and then take us all out to tea."

"Biggest toyshop!" squealed Elly. She was so excited she started talking at once and wouldn't stop, but Charlie sat in the corner with his building bricks saying nothing.

"What's the matter, Charlie?" said Mum, after a time.

"Elly's present," said Charlie in a small voice.

"Well, it's Elly's birthday," said Mum, "you get a present for your birthday, it's Elly's turn now."

"I want crayons," said Charlie.

"All right, you can have some, but cheer up and let's all give Elly a nice day," said Mum, "come on."

Charlie had to decide whether to get into an ack or not. An ack is a horrible, cross, disagreeable mood when all you want to say is ACK. But this time he decided against it.

"Can I have a milk shake?" he said.

"Of course," said Mum. So then they were all excited.

But no-one can have been as excited as Miss Myrtle was the next day. She came round straight after breakfast, smiling all over her face.

"Happy birthday, Elly! Good morning, Charlie! Hello, Robin! Thank heaven it isn't snowing," she said, "are we off?"

"In a minute," said Mum. As soon as they all had put on their coats and hats and boots and gloves and scarves, they said goodbye to Robin (who was absolutely furious at being left behind), and they walked down to the bus stop.

Miss Myrtle was almost embarrassing in the bus. She was making so much noise that the other passengers kept turning round and smiling at her.

"It's years and years since I've been to that toyshop," she said, "ooh, I am looking forward to it! I want to see the costume dolls. I like dolls very much indeed."

Some of the people on the bus were giggling at her—in a nice way, but Elly still wished she'd be a bit quieter.

"What do *you* want, Elly?" said Mum.

"Don't know," said Elly, "maybe a puppet."

Batty's, the toyshop, was in the middle of town but they were very soon there. It was the biggest shop Charlie and Elly had ever been in. "Bigger than Mr Patel's," said Elly, and they all laughed because Mr Patel's little shop seemed a long way away. When they got inside they almost didn't know where to look because there were so many toys everywhere, shelves and shelves of them; toys on big tables, toys on the floor—and Batty's had three floors, so you could go upstairs and downstairs and find even more toys.

"Let's try not to lose each other," said Mum, "but if anybody gets separated from the others, they should go to the teashop over there and then we'll all be able to find them. Have you understood that, Charlie?"

"Yes," said Charlie, insulted. *He* never got lost.

So they started looking round. On the ground floor were shelves with every kind of car and van, lots of bright colours, and all in big boxes. Charlie and Elly liked the cars and vans, but the puppets were even better.

"Donald Duck!" observed Charlie with a squeak. Lots of the puppets were made of wood.

"I bet Sailor could make puppets if he wanted to," said Miss Myrtle, "Sailor can make anything out of wood if he really wants to." But although Sailor actually made flutes and whistles when he was travelling round the world, he never made puppets or dolls.

"I wish he would," said Charlie wistfully.

Some of the puppets in Batty's had been on television too.

"Look at the pig!" squealed Elly. "She's got real diamonds!"

You could play with some of them. Charlie got a glove puppet lion on his hand and growled at Elly's string puppet mouse.

"Go away," said Elly, but the lion wouldn't. He made a grab for the mouse and caught its strings.

"Careful, Charlie," said Mum.

"Look what I've found!" said Miss Myrtle, from the other side of the table. Miss Myrtle had an enormous string puppet clown which was as tall as Charlie. It had a mouth that moved, so you could make it talk.

"Hello, Charlie," it said, "come here a minute." Charlie ran round to see the clown.

"Look at *me*," said the clown, and it bent down and put its hands on the ground and walked on all fours like Robin the dog. Charlie tried to pat it, and it stood up again quickly.

"What's the difference between an elephant and a letter-box?" said the clown.

"Don't know," said Charlie.

"Not much good sending *you* to post a letter then, tee hee hee," said the clown.

"Does anyone want to buy anything?" said the saleslady.

"Not just yet," said Mum. They put the puppets down and went upstairs.

At the top of the stairs was a woman with a monkey in her arms. It was a toy monkey but it looked very real, it was another kind of puppet. It leaned down and put its head on one side to look at Elly.

"Nice monkey," Elly said, but she was a bit scared. The monkey rubbed its soft head against her cheek.

"Aaah," said Elly. It was very cuddly. Then Charlie had a cuddle too. They were in the part of Batty's that only had soft toys: koalas and lions, bears and pandas, leopards, a cross-looking pink hippopotamus, enormous woolly lambs, and big-

gest of all, a donkey on wheels that was half as high as Mum.

"That's the biggest toy I've ever seen," said Elly. She and Charlie had goes at sitting on it and Mum pushed them a little way. Then they went a bit further into the soft toy department, and saw a great heap of green furry frogs all lying on top of each other. They were lovely frogs and not all squidgy like real ones.

"I want one," said Elly.

"You can have one, but wait till you've seen everything and then decide," said Miss Myrtle. She had found her costume dolls, and was standing in front of a glass case full of very grandly-dressed ones.

"It's supposed to be the Royal Family," she said.

"They all look exactly the same," said Mum.

"They're not very good," Miss Myrtle agreed, "and I like most dolls, usually."

They walked on through the computer game place then. Some teenagers were gathered round four or five television screens that made bipping noises, but Charlie and Elly weren't interested. It was getting to be time for tea.

"Have you seen what you want, Elly?" asked Miss Myrtle.

"Don't know," said Elly, "green frog or puppet."

"Have a look on this floor, then make your mind up," said Miss Myrtle.

To everyone's surprise, Elly ended up by choosing a paint box with bottles of special paint that you could put onto wooden things, like Charlie's bricks, or plastic things, like the boat Elly had been given for her birthday. It was a wonderful paint box with eight different colours and three brushes and lots of pictures in the lid. Miss Myrtle paid for it and said, "Happy birthday, Elly!" Then she got some wax crayons for Charlie, then she said, "I'll see you in the tea place"—and then she disappeared.

Mum and Elly and Charlie went and ordered milk shakes and biscuits, and they sat and ate them and talked about what they'd seen, but Miss Myrtle didn't come to meet them.

"I expect she's just gone for a wee," said Mum. But after another milk shake each, Miss Myrtle still hadn't turned up.

"That's funny," said Mum. "I said if anyone got lost to find the tea place, and she said she was coming here anyway. I think we'd better go and look for her."

They looked among the cars and vans and they looked among the puppets, but Miss Myrtle wasn't there. So they tramped off upstairs again, with the parcels. They were quite tired by this time. The monkey waved at them but they weren't in the mood to talk to it, and they walked past the woolly lambs and the cross hippo and the donkey on wheels and the frog heap and the foxy foxes and the furry worms—almost without looking at any of them.

Where *could* she be? Charlie went off exploring on his own. He was good at finding people, he always did well at hide-and-seek. He looked behind some shelves with knights in armour and forts, but she wasn't there. Then he went to where the building bricks were, great piles of them like in the builders' yard Mick sometimes took them to see.

And now Charlie didn't know where to look. He had expected to find Miss Myrtle quite quickly. He wondered where Mum and Elly were, and if he ought to go back and look for them instead. But then something made him think of looking just a bit more, where the computer games were, and he found his way back to Miss Myrtle.

She was sitting in front of one of the screens playing with buttons that operated a football match.

"Miss Myrtle!" Charlie shouted.

"Shush!" said Miss Myrtle, without looking round. "Low energy," she muttered, pressing another button. "Five morale points . . . Desperate midfield attack."

She was so involved in the game that Charlie couldn't even make her turn round. Some of the teenagers were finding it very funny.

"Up the greens!" shouted Miss Myrtle. She was playing two teams, green and blue. Charlie went and found Mum and Elly.

"Miss Myrtle's playing football and she won't stop,"
he said. Mum hurried to the computer game place.
Several of the teenagers had stopped playing; the sight
of an eighty-year-old lady playing computer football
was better than their own games.

"Defend, greens, come *on!*" shouted Miss Myrtle.

"Come on, Miss Myrtle, we've got to get home or
the buses will all be full," said Mum.

"One more game and I'll have finished those blues,"
said Miss Myrtle, "they're weakening now, no staying
power . . ."

"Please," said Mum.

"Oh all right," said Miss Myrtle, and she stood up
grumpily. "Missed my tea, I suppose," she said.

"'Fraid so," said Mum.

"You sure about the buses?" said Miss Myrtle.

"Absolutely," said Mum.

All the way home no-one could hear themselves speak, because Miss Myrtle and Elly were talking so loudly. Listening to the two of them, you couldn't be sure whose birthday treat it had been.

Jackson and the
Pond

Jackson, the fourteen-year-old punk, was one of Charlie and Elly's best friends. He lived across the road from them, and *he* said his spiky hair and torn clothes looked fashionable, but practically everybody else said they looked silly. Mrs Rotten always said Jackson was a disgrace and ought to be ashamed of himself, which he most certainly was not.

Still, Jackson did look a bit of a mess, and both Dad and Mum had suggested more than once that he might tidy himself up a bit. "What for?" was his answer, and neither Mum nor Dad could think of anything to say after that, particularly because Jackson was actually very nice and gentle, and a good friend of Charlie and Elly. They often went on adventures together and, after all, not many teenagers bother to make friends with little children of four and five.

One freezing winter's day Jackson dropped in to see if Charlie and Elly wanted to go to the park. "No!" said Charlie at once. Robin barked a lot and jumped up and down, which meant yes. It was a funny thing about Robin's tail that it went round in circles when he wagged it, and not from side to side like most other tails. And this time Robin's tail went round so fast that he almost looked like a helicopter!

"Yes, yes, Jackson!" said Elly, "come *on*, Charlie," she said.

"Go on, Charlie," said Mum, "the others want to go, you'll like it when you get outside, the pond might be frozen."

"No." Charlie was a very determined person and once he had made his mind up, it usually stayed made up. "I'm building," he said. He was making a station out of wooden bricks.

"Oh *go* on, Charlie," said Elly again, and Robin came skipping round him, whirring his tail just above his station, and he accidentally knocked the whole thing over with his back leg.

"WAAA!" squawked Charlie, very upset.

"Come on, that settles it," said Mum. And in no time at all she had got Charlie and Elly into their coats and hats and boots and gloves and scarves, and they were all bundling out of the house. It wasn't far to the

park, but they had to go very slowly because the pavement was all slidy and they were slipping all over the place.

"I don't care if I slip," Jackson said, "it's nothing, you get up again. I fell down on the football pitch four times last Tuesday and it was really icy and I could've broken my legs."

"Don't believe you," said Elly, who knew Jackson's tales. Elly was good at seeing through people.

"Nearly took all the skin off my knee, anyway," said Jackson.

"Show us!" said Charlie.

"Oh well, it's better now, nothing to see is there?" said Jackson.

"Don't believe you," said Elly again, "Dad says you make things up all the time."

"Want a bet?" said Jackson.

But by this time they were all at the park gates. Robin sat down so they could take his lead off. Then he ran like a rocket to the pond. The children followed more carefully but still quite quickly, and very soon they were at the pond—and it *was* frozen!

The pond was frozen right across, and Robin thought it was the same as the snowy grass and went running straight on to it. He got a shock! His feet slipped in all directions and his legs sort of did the splits twice, front and back. He couldn't stop at all. And the look on his face was so furious, you'd have thought Charlie and Elly and Jackson had put the ice there themselves. Mind you, they were all laughing like anything and he wasn't getting any sympathy.

"Robin thought it was the ground!" squeaked Elly.

"What an idiot," said Jackson, "coo Robin, what an idiot! You look really stupid."

Poor Robin was trying his hardest to get off the ice, but every time he tried to pick up his legs to start walking again, they slid away from him; and if he managed to take a couple of steps properly with his front legs, his back legs would start going sideways and he would fall over. The children were laughing so much that they fell over too, and rolled on top of the icy grass. Jackson, who normally would have helped Charlie and Elly to stand up, was doubled up with laughter himself.

"Don't stop, Robin," he spluttered between giggles, "please don't stop," and for ages Robin didn't stop, but at last it began to look as though he had worked out how to walk on the ice and he began to plod very carefully back. He slipped a few more times before he got back to the side, but it had all been too much for Jackson. He had to get on the ice as well, even though there was a sign to say that you mustn't.

Jackson went slithering off towards the middle of the pond where there was a little island. He meant to make a slide, the sort you could run up to and get a really long slide on—not all over the place like Robin, but a proper one where *you* decide how long to slide for, and you don't fall over. So Jackson went to look for a good strong bit of ice (which he could see by the colour) and he began to work the slide, which you do by sliding in the same place enough times to make it smooth.

But he'd had only two or three goes before one of the park keepers came up and shouted at him to get off.

"Go on, mister, just let me have five minutes, what's it to you?" pleaded Jackson.

"It's the rules, that's what it is to me," said the park keeper.

"I hate parkies," said Jackson softly, but he came off the ice all the same. Charlie and Elly were quite glad to see him.

"You might have fallen in," said Elly.

"Nah," said Jackson, "it's dead strong, that. It held Robin, didn't it? Where *is* Robin?"

They all looked round.

"He's gone off," said Charlie.

"He's not speaking to us," said Elly. At that moment Robin came back to see them but he wasn't very friendly at all. He hadn't liked skating and being laughed at. They all said "Hello Robin," and "Are you all right?" but he was in a real sulk. And so was Jackson. His hands were stuck right down in his pockets and his shoulders were hunched up, and he was kicking at the ice on the ground. Jackson in a mood was no fun at all.

"I'm going back on the ice!" Jackson said suddenly. "I don't care what some stupid parky says, it's good on the ice," and he raced off before anyone could say anything. Charlie and Elly went back towards the pond feeling worried. The ice might not be very strong and

Jackson was in a silly mood. When they got there, Jackson was already sliding again.

"Look everybody, it's terrific!" he said. "It's really good! Wheeeee—" CRACK! What they had all been afraid of really happened, and Jackson fell in the pond. Luckily it wasn't very deep, but it was muddy and very, very cold.

At first Charlie and Elly thought it was quite funny, like when Robin had been slipping all over, but in a minute or two when Jackson had hardly moved, things began to look frightening. The children were getting cold, Robin just stood there looking stupid, and Jackson went on struggling without getting out. Though the water was only up to his waist, he couldn't move at all.

"Stuck," he said, in a squeaky little voice that didn't sound like him.

"Come out," said Elly bravely, but she was frightened too. "Come on, Jackson!"

"It's all muddy, my feet are stuck," squeaked Jackson, but he tried a bit harder to find something on the ice to hold with his hands and pull himself out.

Charlie and Elly burst into tears at exactly the same moment, something they didn't often do.

Luckily for all of them, George the parky had made a very good guess at where Jackson's mood might take him. He stumped off round the park thinking, "I bet that silly blooming lad goes back on the pond." He thought it a bit more and then he thought, "Best go and see what that stupid punk's got up to." And so he

stumped back to the pond. When he got there, he was furious!

"You stupid little git!" he shouted at Jackson, "what did I tell you? Out!"

"Stuck," said Jackson, in a very small voice. Then George noticed that Charlie and Elly were crying.

"Oh blimey," he muttered. "Hang on, you two," he said to Charlie and Elly, "don't cry, I'll get him out," and he went and fetched a very long pole and his own very long wellington boots.

"Catch hold of the pole," he said to Jackson. "QUICK!" He had to shout because by this time Jackson had got too cold to think properly.

Jackson grabbed the pole and the park keeper pulled it, but Jackson still couldn't move. In the end, to get him out, George had to put on the very long wellingtons and break the ice and go into the water himself.

He found that Jackson's legs were tangled in some branches, so he cleared them. Then he almost had to carry Jackson, who by now was freezing. Charlie and Elly were still quite upset, and Robin's tail was extremely droopy.

"You'd better come back to my house and have tea," said George.

So they did. They were a gloomy little crowd as they trudged across the park.

The park keeper's house was behind a high hedge and the children had often wondered what it might look like inside. When they got in, they found the rooms were tiny and full of dark furniture, but there were lots of lights and a real log fire and it all looked very cosy. Charlie and Elly began to cheer up very soon but poor Jackson was still quite upset.

"You go and get in a hot bath," said the parky to Jackson, "and you two kids sit by the fire and I'll get you some tea."

So Charlie and Elly and Robin sat by the fire while George showed Jackson where the bathroom was. Jackson had a bath and came down in George's dressing gown, and soon they were all warm, and the parky brought tea and biscuits.

"We got frightened," said Elly.

And Charlie said, "Jackson was stuck, wasn't he, his legs were stuck, he was all cold."

The park keeper thought this was the moment to tell them off, but then he looked at Charlie and Elly's faces, just starting to get pink again, and he didn't.

"You shouldn't play on the ice," said George. Then he said to Jackson, "When you're out with the kids, don't muck about like that." And that was all.

"Robin can catch!" announced Charlie, to change the subject. Charlie could throw very well, like when he hit Mrs Rotten with the snowball. He threw a biscuit to Robin and Robin caught it. They all started to play with Robin, and even poor Jackson began to join in. Jackson could throw a biscuit in the air and catch it in his own mouth. "Look, mister," he said to the park keeper, and did it.

"Oh well, throwing biscuits in the air, I suppose everybody's got to be good at something," said George ungraciously. Jackson did it several more times, just to get back into favour. Then it was time to go home.

"You lot will have to clear off now, I got work to do," said the parky, though really he had enjoyed having the children to tea, very much.

But there was one more problem: Jackson's jeans

weren't dry yet. He borrowed some of the parky's trousers which were miles too big for him, so the legs had to be rolled up and Jackson had to hold the tops up with his hands. He did look funny!

Jackson got a terrible telling off when they all got back to Charlie and Elly's house, and a much worse one when he got back to his own house. His mum and dad said he had been very silly to go on the ice. He was in even more trouble because he should have been looking after Charlie and Elly. Sailor was round at Jackson's house and although he didn't say anything, his face showed that, for once, he wasn't on Jackson's side.

But one good thing came out of it: George the parky was a new friend, and they saw him lots and lots after that.

Charlie and Elly and the Kennel

It was a bright day in early spring, and everything in Charlie and Elly's garden was looking lovely. Lots of daffodils were out, and gorgeous-smelling white narcissi, and orange and red wallflowers. The leaves on the trees at the end of the garden were unfolding. They were a very light green which went almost yellow when the sun shone through them. Spring green, Miss Myrtle called it, and she said it was magic.

But even though it was all so pretty, and even though the sun was out, Charlie and Elly were in a real ack. Usually, when you're in an ack, you end up being not very nice, and the children weren't being at all nice that day.

"Your feet smell, Robin," said Elly, "ooh, they stink, your feet, poo."

Poor Robin felt very miserable. He never really got acky himself. He went up to Charlie, wagging his tail round and round in the helicopter way, but Charlie just ignored him and started doing cartwheels. Charlie was very good at acrobatics. Robin felt there was nothing much for him to do there, so he took himself off down to the trees and hung about on his own.

Just then, Dad came out of the house carrying some wood and a hammer, and Charlie and Elly ran up to him yelling very loud.

"Play with us, Dad, go on play with us!" said Charlie.

"We're all acky," explained Elly. Robin ran back from the trees, wagging his tail hopefully. But Dad just said, "Not now," which wasn't like him.

"What are you doing with the wood?" asked Elly, who was always very practical. She said it in a rather anxious way because Dad was totally hopeless at making things.

"Surprise," said Dad, with a funny little grin.

"What is it?" said Charlie and Elly together, but Dad only grinned a bit more.

"TELL US!" they shrieked, but there was no answer.

Dad looked very pleased with himself. He went back to the house and came back again with some more wood, and then he went back again and came out with boxes of nails. Dad began to nail pieces of wood together and as usual he kept bashing his fingers with the hammer by mistake; but although he kept shouting "Bother" and "Sugar" and "Heaven's sake", his very good humour stayed with him and the little smile at the corners of his mouth was fixed on as if it had been glued. When he spoke to the children at all, it was extremely silly and very ack-making indeed.

"*Tell us what it is!*" Charlie shrieked.

"Wednesday," Dad said.

"What you're doing," said Elly.

"Hammering," said Dad. "ow!"

It was quite hopeless. The children tried to guess what the wooden thing was.

"I know, it's a place to put spades in," said Elly. Dad didn't answer.

"It is, isn't it. Tell us!" Dad still didn't answer, he just kept grinning and banging his fingers.

"It's a box to keep our coal in," Elly suggested. Dad still wouldn't say anything.

"Just tell us yes or no," Elly pleaded. Then Charlie thought of the answer.

"Going to be a sandpit, like in the park!" he shouted.

"A sandpit!" Elly squealed. What a brilliant idea. The wooden sides must be for holding sand in.

"I can make castles," said Charlie.

"I can make them too," said Elly. Robin came running up, and bounced around, trying to get the children to play. "Robin might dig the sand up," said Elly, and Robin wagged his tail.

But however hard they tried they couldn't get Dad to say for certain what the wooden thing was going to be, and so after a while they went off down to the trees to play tig with Robin. Their hearts weren't in it, they couldn't stop hearing the hammering, so when Miss Myrtle appeared in her garden they ran eagerly over to the fence. Robin went too.

"Hello, Charlie and Elly and Robin!" said Miss Myrtle. "What a racket! Whatever's your dad up to?"

"We don't *know*!" they shouted. Elly tried to explain.

"He's making something out of wood but he won't say what it is. He's been banging nails in with a hammer. He's been banging them from when we had breakfast. They're big nails and he keeps banging his fingers . . . What do you think it is?"

"Oh, I don't know," said Miss Myrtle, peering over the fence. The wooden thing seemed to have four sides now, like a very shallow box without a top.

"Maybe it's a kennel for Robin," said Miss Myrtle.

"What's a kennel?" asked Charlie.

"It's a house for a dog to live in," explained Miss Myrtle.

Robin looked very miserable. His head hung down and his tail stopped wagging, and he sat on the grass looking from Elly to Miss Myrtle and back again. Elly said, "But Robin sleeps under the stairs in his big bed on Charlie's jumper! Oh Robin, you can't live in a kennel!"

Robin looked more miserable than ever.

"Perhaps it isn't a kennel," said Miss Myrtle, wishing she hadn't said anything. "No, it can't be, it's too big," she went on, and from what they could see it was going to be very much too big, but Charlie and Elly and Robin could not be comforted. They all got gloomier and gloomier and Miss Myrtle quickly said, "Come on everybody, let's go and have some cake! Quick!" which cheered everyone up. They ran into Miss Myrtle's house for cake, but they soon came out again. They couldn't think of anything but the banging noise.

They all went over to the fence.

"We could stay here and watch for a bit," suggested Miss Myrtle. Charlie and Elly climbed on Miss Myrtle's bench so they could see over the fence, and Miss Myrtle just stood. The wooden thing wasn't all that much bigger, it didn't reach as high as Dad's waist yet. They watched and were quiet for an incredibly long time, nearly three minutes. Then they began to play I-spy, in very soft voices.

Poor Dad was terribly put off. He pretended not to notice because they were all being so quiet, but the trouble was that hopeless as he was at making things, he was much, much worse when he was being watched. Dad began to bash his hands more often, by mistake, then he'd swear more loudly, and then he'd mutter "Sorry" under his breath.

Charlie and Elly and Miss Myrtle started to find this very funny, and from laughing just a bit they really got the giggles, so that everything Dad did made them giggle more and more. It got so bad that Dad was about to send them all away, but then he dropped the big hammer on his foot.

"ow!" he yelled, hopping sideways. "GET OFF THAT BLOOMING FENCE!" he shouted at Charlie and Elly, but they were laughing so much they had to hold on to the fence so as not to fall off Miss Myrtle's bench.

"Tee hee hee hee hee hee, tee hee hee hee hee," they went, almost choking. Dad was still hopping but getting crosser all the time, and he tripped on the nail box and went flying backwards into a corner of the wooden

thing, pushing two of its walls over. Those two walls took the other two with them and the whole thing collapsed, with Dad lying in the middle.

Charlie and Elly very nearly did fall off Miss Myrtle's bench, they were laughing so much. Miss Myrtle was laughing quite a bit too, but she managed to hold on to them long enough to help them down. It was very mean to be giggling when Dad was in such trouble, but they couldn't help it. Robin went through the gate to see what had happened, found Dad lying dazed and upset surrounded by bits of wood, and went and leaned his warm, furry self against Dad for comfort.

In a couple of minutes Dad had got up again and was looking hopelessly at the wooden mess all round him when Miss Myrtle's doorbell rang. It was Sailor! Sailor might make everything all right again, he was not only brilliant at making things out of wood but also at calming people's nerves.

"Can I help?" he offered, when he went through the gate between the gardens and saw the ruin. "I was working on Mr Patel's roof and I saw the whole thing. Are you all right?"

"Oh Sailor, I'm all right, but I think I've wrecked my building," said Dad in a very miserable voice.

"We'll see about that," said Sailor, "it may not be as wrecked as you think. I could help you put it back together but I need to know what it was going to be."

"It was going to be a surprise!" wailed Dad, almost in tears.

"I can't build surprises," said Sailor gently.

"It was a play house for the children and Robin," said Dad.

"A play house!" said Charlie and Elly together. They couldn't take it in at first. Then they got more and more excited. "A PLAY HOUSE!!!" They could hardly believe it. "Charlie and Elly can help us build it," said Sailor, which is what they did.

Charlie and Elly picked up all the nails and collected the bits of wood that weren't broken. Dad showed Sailor the drawing he'd been working from and Sailor suggested one or two changes. Then they all set to work, Sailor telling everybody what to do. Elly was especially good at organizing things, so she had to sort out the nails and tools and keep them in order when people were using them. Charlie was best at holding things straight for people to see, and he could even knock nails in properly if somebody watched to make sure. Dad went and got some special stuff for the roof. And all the time Sailor worked very, very fast.

"You're getting on like a *house on fire*, Sailor," said Dad, when he came back with the roof stuff. Sailor just groaned and carried on, which you often had to with Dad's jokes.

Meanwhile Robin and Miss Myrtle had disappeared. When Sailor came round Miss Myrtle knew the wooden thing would get built, so just in case it really was going to be a kennel she took Robin into her house for a bit. The others were working too hard to notice.

After several hours of holding and hammering and running to fetch things, the play house was finished. It was wonderful! It had two windows (without glass) and a doorway without a door. It even had a bench and a table inside. Charlie and Elly could hardly believe how wonderful it was.

"Where's Robin?" said Charlie suddenly.

"Haven't seen him for ages," said Dad.

"Maybe he's with Miss Myrtle," said Sailor, who always seemed to guess things somehow. So Charlie ran to the fence and shouted and shouted, but it was a long time before Robin came out. He walked terribly slowly, with his head down and his tail drooping. He still thought it might be a kennel.

"Look, Robin! It's our play house!" Elly squealed.

Robin stood absolutely still for a minute and then launched himself at it like a rocket. He jumped in and out of the window frames and he ran into the house and then out of it, and then round and round it, and then he jumped on the bench. And then everybody was happy, Charlie and Elly and Robin and Dad and Sailor—and Miss Myrtle, too. *She* was happy because everybody else was—and because the doorway was just big enough for her to go through, if she bent down. All this time, Sailor and Dad couldn't stop grinning at how pleased they were with their work.

Then it was time for Miss Myrtle and Sailor to go.

"Bye-bye, Charlie and Elly," they said.

"Come and see us in our new house tomorrow," said Charlie and Elly.

woof said Robin.

Charlie and Elly
at the Fair

On May Day morning Miss Myrtle went to her garden fence to look for Charlie and Elly, but they weren't there.

This was very odd. Charlie and Elly played in their garden nearly all the time, and almost whatever the weather. Where could they be? Miss Myrtle felt rather put out. They hadn't told her anything yesterday about being away. She went indoors and came out again in an hour and they *still* weren't there. It was lunchtime, so she went and had something to eat. And so the day went on, Miss Myrtle looking out for Charlie and Elly from time to time, and Charlie and Elly not being there, until suddenly at teatime there was an awful lot of noise.

"Hello Miss Myrtle, guess where *we*'ve been!" Charlie and Elly shouted.

"I've no idea, you never told me," said Miss Myrtle, who was feeling a bit hurt.

"We've been to the Fair!" they yelled, and when she looked at them properly, Miss Myrtle saw their faces were very dirty and smeary and so were their clothes, and they'd got brightly coloured things in their hands.

Charlie had a plastic bag with a goldfish in it. Elly was hooting a sort of metal trumpet.

"We went on the dodgems"—"I went on the Waltzer but Charlie daredn't"—"Yes I dare"—"No you didn't"—"Well I went on the ghost train *and* the rocket."

They were both talking so fast, they didn't even have time to argue.

"I won the hooking-a-duck thing," said Charlie proudly.

"*Everybody* wins the hooking-a-duck thing," said Elly.

"What fun, you two, tell me everything, what was your favourite?" said Miss Myrtle, who had forgotten about feeling left out.

"Dodgems!" they both shouted.

"Who drove?" said Miss Myrtle.

"We both did," said Elly. "I drove first. A big boy kept crashing into us, but Mum told him to stop and he did."

"Amazing!" said Miss Myrtle.

"I drove the red car!" said Charlie. "It went fastest! I bumped lots of cars!"

"You're not supposed to," said Elly.

"Yes you are," said Charlie.

"Never mind all that, what happened after the dodgems?" said Miss Myrtle.

"We saw Jackson," said Elly, "but he didn't talk much."

"Well, I expect he was with his friends," said Miss Myrtle. She was right. Jackson had been with some of his friends and they'd been having fun and getting shouted at, standing up on the dodgems and things. Mum had said, "Hello Jackson," and Jackson had said, "Hello, got to go now." But the next person they bumped into was more friendly: it was Mick the builder, with two of his children.

"Mick was going to look after Charlie, but Charlie got lost first," Elly said.

"That was good," said Charlie.

"Gracious me, Charlie, whatever do you mean?" said Miss Myrtle. She couldn't think how being lost could be good.

"I tied the man up," explained Charlie.

"WHAT?" said Miss Myrtle.

"Mick was looking at the Waltzer but Charlie just walked off," Elly broke in.

"I saw the goldfish where the darts were but I couldn't find Mick."

"Then you started to cry," said Elly.

"Didn't," said Charlie.

"Did," said Elly.

"Come on, Charlie, get on with it," said Miss Myrtle.

"A lady with a hat came, she had all blue clothes on."

"Was that a policewoman?" asked Miss Myrtle.

"No," said Charlie, "a lost lady."

"Ambulance lady," Elly remarked helpfully.

"Oh, it must have been the St John's Ambulance," said Miss Myrtle. "What about you, Elly, were you worried about Charlie?"

"Course we were," said Elly, who didn't look it. "We went looking for him, then Mum said, 'Let's go to the ambulance place', but he didn't want to come out."

Charlie was laughing and giggling as he thought about it.

"I tied the man up!" he said again.

And Miss Myrtle said "What?" again—this part of the story wasn't getting any better.

"He means the ambulance man," said Elly, who was getting a bit bored with talking about Charlie. "Charlie put bandage all on the ambulance man," she explained.

"Oh Charlie, terrific!" said Miss Myrtle, who understood these things, and she asked lots of questions and slowly managed to piece together what had happened.

It turned out that Charlie had had a stupendous time in the St John's Ambulance tent. Everybody had made a big fuss of him and one of the nurses had let him play with the instruments used for helping people who were ill—all the ones that weren't too sharp, anyway. Then he'd found a box of bandages and the nurse had said, "Why not put the ambulanceman's arm in a sling?" Charlie had gone a bit berserk.

"I put it on his arm and his neck and his head and his legs," Charlie said dreamily. The poor ambulanceman hadn't been able to move at all.

"What a nice ambulanceman to let you do all that to him," said Miss Myrtle, thinking to herself that the man must have been batty.

"He didn't want to," said Charlie.

Apparently Charlie was not alone in being carried away by the fun of playing with all the bandages, because the nurse was egging him on and getting more and more bandages out of the cupboard, and the more bandages Charlie tied round the poor ambulanceman, the less funny the man found it. Several times he asked them to undo him, and then he began to get really cross.

"This is ridiculous, we're supposed to be working,"

he said angrily, but the nurse and Charlie went on with it anyway.

Charlie was tying the most peculiar knots because they seemed to make the nurse laugh more. She kept getting more bandage out of the cupboard for Charlie and she was giggling so much she knocked things over.

"Oh Charlie, you're a little star!" she kept saying. The man got crosser and crosser, but now he was completely tied up. Charlie and the nurse put a bandage over his mouth so he couldn't even talk. By that time they were both almost helpless with laughter.

Charlie thought it was quite funny putting so many bandages on somebody, but mostly he was laughing because the nurse was laughing and he seemed to be able to make her laugh more. Then she started tickling him. By this time they were making a horrendous noise with all their giggling and shrieking, and a policeman came in.

"What's going on?" he said. The nurse went on shrieking but Charlie went very quiet.

The policeman stared for a moment at the shrieking nurse, the tied-up, gagged ambulanceman and the silent child.

"Everything all right?" he said. The nurse was at that stage of the giggles when you really can't stop, and everything anybody says makes you giggle even more. All the same she tried to explain.

"It's Charlie!" she began, and went off into another giggling fit.

"What is?" asked the policeman.

"He is," said the nurse, waving wildly round the room. It was ages and ages before the policeman could find out what was happening and unfortunately, when he did, he started laughing too. The poor ambulanceman's face went purple with fury. Then the nurse started explaining all over again.

"This is Charlie," she said.

"Hello, Charlie."

"He's lost," said the nurse.

"He certainly looks it," said the policeman, pretending to be serious. For some reason the policeman and the nurse started laughing again.

"And why is this person here done up like a *mummy*?" said the policeman. Then he started to giggle some

more. "I think it's *Charlie's mummy!*" he spluttered.
"*Mrs Tutankhamen!*" Charlie didn't see why that was
meant to be funny, but the nurse and the policeman
roared with laughter.

Then the policeman got serious again and he said,
"I think I'd better release the prisoner," and he began
to undo the ambulanceman, who was furious. His face
was still red and he looked a very ugly look.

"This whole ridiculous incident will be reported,"
he said. "It's absolutely ridiculous! You've brought the
Service into ridiculousness! You're for it!"

In the middle of this, when the last bandages were
coming off, Mum and Elly turned up.

"Oh Charlie, thank heaven you're all right, whatever
made you wander off like that?" Mum said. And Elly
said crossly, "We've looked all over for you." Mum
gave Charlie a big hug and a kiss, but all Charlie said
was, "Want to stay and play." Mum was a bit fed up.

"Has he been good?" she asked the ambulanceman.

"No! He has not, madam!" shouted the ambulanceman. "But it wasn't entirely his fault."

"Oh dear," said Mum.

"Gross misconduct," said the ambulanceman.

"Charlie!" said Mum.

"I expect you'll be going now," said the ambulanceman in a stern voice.

"Not going!" said Charlie.

Elly told this bit of the story to Miss Myrtle.

"He didn't want to come out at all," she said, "then
Mum said he could have candyfloss *and* a goldfish."

You could see Elly was getting into an ack about this. She'd been very good all day, after all, and not tied anybody up, and then Charlie was the one getting all the presents.

But Miss Myrtle still wanted to hear lots more about the Fair and she said, "What a wonderful day you've had! Do you want to come and have a drink of orange and tell me some more?"

"YES!" said the children, and Elly forgot her ackiness. They went into Miss Myrtle's house talking louder and faster than before.

"When I won hooking-a-duck I got a sailor puppet" —"Look at my trumpet!"—"The big wheel, you can see the top of the church from it and you can see everything and it makes you feel sick"—"The nurse said I was clever but the bandage man said he was going to bandage *me* one day."

Charlie and Elly never stopped talking until supper.

Charlie and Elly's Visitor

One day, when spring was turning to summer, Charlie and Elly went into their garden. Robin the dog was barking at the door of their play house, so they ran up to see what was the matter. The play house didn't have a door, you just walked straight in. It didn't have windows either, and sometimes Robin just jumped straight out!

"What is it, Robin?" asked Elly.

"Robin's woofing lots and lots," remarked Charlie.

Robin didn't usually make such a fuss about the play house, but this time he went on and on barking and looking inside it. When Charlie and Elly came up to the doorway, they saw at once what he was barking at.

In the far corner, between the bench and the table, was an animal. It wasn't very big, and it looked frightened. It had a big bushy tail and beady eyes, and it was a sort of rusty colour. Elly said, "I think it's a squirrel." Then she thought they'd better send Robin away. "Robin, go and play in the trees," she said. Robin wouldn't go at first, until Elly said it again, very fiercely. Then he did.

"Will it bite?" said Charlie, looking at the squirrel.

"I don't know," said Elly, "I s'pose it might." They were quite scared, but then the squirrel ran forward with two or three quick little steps and it looked so nice and furry they thought it would be all right to make friends with it.

"Let's give it something to eat," said Elly, and Charlie got a piece of apple out of his pocket and threw it on the floor by the squirrel. The squirrel grabbed the apple in its paws really quickly, with funny, nervous little movements. It held the apple between its paws, so that the apple poked out of the top and looked a bit like a boiled egg looks when it's held in an egg cup. The squirrel began to nibble at the apple straight away.

"Oh *good*," said Elly, who was beginning to like this visitor very much. "Get some more, Charlie."

Charlie had to go indoors for more apple, and he got Mum to cut one up for him. By the time he got back the squirrel had jumped up on to the table and Elly was very excited.

"Look, look!" she said, "it likes us!"

Charlie was excited too but still a bit scared, though he was determined not to show it. He went very quietly into the play house, sat down on the bench, and put another bit of apple on the table for the squirrel. The squirrel sat looking at him out of its little black shiny eyes. It was very pretty, with a pointed face, and the fur around its ears was fine, like feathers. Its big tail seemed to be able to move in any direction. But just at this moment the squirrel was quite still, staring and staring at Charlie, only its beady eyes seemed to flicker sometimes as though it was trying to look all round.

Suddenly the squirrel darted forward to pick up the apple, grabbed it, and ate it up very quickly. Then it saw that Charlie had more apple in his hand, so it jumped on to his lap! And by now Charlie wasn't frightened at all, but very excited! He still knew somehow that he must keep still so as not to frighten the squirrel away, but it was quite hard for him. He wanted to stroke it and play with it. The squirrel sat eating the rest of the apple and it seemed very happy to be there. Elly wished it was sitting on *her* lap.

"You are lucky, Charlie," she said. A real live squirrel getting that close! Elly wondered if they might stay friends with it so it could come back and sit on her lap.

But then something awful happened. Robin ran up to the play house door. He was at his very noisiest, barking and whining and jumping—he wanted to play. Elly shouted, "Go away, Robin! Shut up!" but it was much too late. Robin had seen the squirrel and the squirrel had seen Robin. Robin rushed up to it, barking, and the squirrel was so frightened that it ran down Charlie's legs and then stopped still, on the floor. Robin had his front legs on the floor as though he was lying down, but his back legs standing up and his bottom in the air. His tail was wagging slightly. This sometimes meant he wanted to play, and it sometimes meant he wanted to fight. No-one could guess which it was, least of all the squirrel, which must have been terrified because the next thing it did was to run back up

Charlie's leg again. Robin stood up suddenly and seemed about to put his front legs on Charlie's knee.

"ow!" screamed Charlie. "ow ow ow ow ow ow ow!"

The squirrel had bitten his arm.

Elly was sometimes so brilliant at organizing things that it almost took your breath away. She took charge of this situation at once. First, she banged her fist on the table to shoo the squirrel away, and she chased it out of the window. This wasn't difficult because the squirrel was very frightened by this time, and mad keen to go. Next, Elly turned on Robin.

"GET OUT!" she yelled, in a voice that sent him straight down to the trees. Then she went to Charlie and gave him a big hug. "Come and find Mum," she said. Charlie was still upset. He was crying a bit, but more from fright than anything. The squirrel hadn't really bitten him deeply, it was just a nip, but scary all the same. Charlie got up and went indoors with Elly.

Mum wasn't there when they got inside but it was all right because Dad was, so he looked after them. Even though Charlie's bite wasn't bad, Dad took both the children very quickly to the doctor to make sure. The doctor wasn't far away, just across the park, so they walked there. On the way they met Mrs Rotten talking to George the parky.

"Squirrel bit me," said Charlie.

"What rotten luck," said Mrs Rotten, which made everyone laugh. Mrs Rotten was really called something quite ordinary like Brown or Hall, but she'd been called Mrs Rotten for such a long time that no-one could remember what her real name was.

"Why are you laughing?" she asked.

"Not laughing," said Charlie, laughing.

"Good luck at the doctor's," said George the parky, and he bent down and gave Charlie a hug.

Charlie was all right, really, but he loved all the fuss. The doctor said both children were all right, and they went back home, and Dad gave them some orange and biscuits. They kept telling the story over and over again.

"Robin frightened it," said Elly, for the twentieth time.

"It was eating apple and then it bit me," Charlie said, for the fiftieth time.

"We wanted to make friends," said Elly sadly.

"You might still be able to make friends," said Dad, "but in a different way."

"How?" asked Charlie.

"Put some more apple pieces out tomorrow," said Dad, "but just put them on the garden wall so the squirrel doesn't have to come down too far. You can reach the top of the wall, can't you?"

"Yes," said Charlie, who could climb it. The wall was at the very end of the garden and it had a flat part on top where you could put things. It joined up the two wooden fences which were at the sides. Charlie was very good at climbing practically anything, so the garden wall was easy for him.

Dad went on, "When you've put the apple on the wall, you'll have to go back into the bushes and wait very very quietly and see if the squirrel will come down for the apple. Don't even think about trying to get the squirrel back into your play house because that would be silly, and anyway it would be too frightened."

"Will it come?" asked Charlie.

"I don't know, it's worth a go," said Dad.

So the next day they did exactly what Dad had said, but the squirrel didn't come. They did it the day after that, and the day after *that*, but still the squirrel didn't come.

Elly said, "Let's not bother, it must have gone away," but Charlie said, "Let's try again," which was odd in a way, since he was the one who had been bitten. Charlie could be very peculiar sometimes. He didn't seem to mind falling over or bashing bits of himself nearly as much as most children did. But he could climb trees and swing on swings and run along walls much better than practically everybody—which maybe had something to do with him not being bothered for very long by the squirrel bite.

So, on the fourth day, they went out again with some more chopped-up apple, and they went down to the trees again. They put the apple on the wall, and then they looked and looked, but still they couldn't see the squirrel. They couldn't even see it high up in the trees.

"The squirrel's gone away," said Elly. "We'll never see it again."

"We *will*," said Charlie fiercely. But he was almost crying.

"Don't cry, Charlie," said Elly, "doesn't matter."

"I'm not," said Charlie, gulping.

They began to walk back to the house, their heads down and their steps very slow and gloomy. Halfway there, Charlie turned round to look at the tree again.

"Elly!" he said in a sort of shouting whisper. "Look!"

Elly turned round and peered at the trees, but she couldn't see anything.

"Look!" squealed Charlie again, pointing. "He's back!"

Elly squinted at where Charlie was pointing, and then she saw it! The squirrel was on the wall where the apple pieces were. It had a piece in its paws and it was eating with the hurried little nibbling movements they remembered so well.

"Squirrel's back, squirrel's back!" Charlie said, laughing with excitement. He stared for a bit longer and then he almost yelled, "It winked at me!"

"No it didn't. Couldn't have. You're silly," Elly said sternly. "Squirrels can't do winking." But you could see that she was thrilled too, really. They watched for a few minutes more, and the squirrel finished and ran back up the tree again.

"Better put more apple out tomorrow," said Elly.

Charlie and Elly
and Mick

Charlie and Elly and Robin—and Mum and Dad—
lived in a nice old house with funny little sets of steps
going into some of the rooms, and funny old windows
that went up and down instead of opening outwards
like most windows do. They all liked it very much.
It was almost exactly like Miss Myrtle's house, and
Sailor's, and Jackson's, and Mrs Rotten's—in fact, like
all the other houses in the street.

The houses were even older than Miss Myrtle. Miss
Myrtle was eighty and she had lived in her house for
sixty years, but the houses were more than a hundred
years old. With houses as old as that, it was not
surprising that things often needed to be mended and
patched up. That summer it was the turn of Charlie
and Elly's roof.

Mick the builder came to mend the roof, and from
the minute he arrived he was Charlie and Elly's great
friend. He was quite young, and he laughed a lot and
teased them. He would make funny bird noises from
the roof, or imitate Robin. "Woof woof!" he barked,
loud as anything. Charlie and Elly barked back at him,
looking up from the window. Robin thought Mick was

silly and Robin was absolutely right, judging from his conversations.

"I've had me vest on for three weeks now and it's stuck to me," said Mick. "You'll have to get it off with a hammer and chisel if you're wanting it off at all."

"You haven't," said Elly.

"Well, and how would you know about it either way?" said Mick.

"You can't have."

"It's stuck on, same as me boots. I've had them on for three weeks and all. You can't get those off now, can you?"

This sort of talk could go on for ages, getting sillier and sillier, but no-one could get sillier than Mick, it was impossible. The stuck-on boots conversation ended with him asking the children to polish them.

"I'm going out tonight and I've got to look like a film star," he said.

"There's all mud on your boots," Charlie pointed out.

"You can't do polish on top of mud," said Elly.

"Well, now I'll never be a film star," said Mick, "and I'll tell them it was all because of you."

Charlie and Elly did lots of the things that Mick was doing. When Mick started hammering, the children started hammering as well. When Mick sang silly songs, Charlie and Elly sang back at him. It was good fun. Mick was always saying things about other people that Charlie and Elly weren't allowed to say. "That Mrs Rotten, she's got a mouth on her would look a lot better on a letter-box," or "You can't help seeing a lot of Jackson, can you, there's so many holes in his clothes."

One afternoon Mick found that he'd run out of sand.

"Can Charlie and Elly come with me to the yard for some sand, Mrs?" he asked Mum.

"Of course," said Mum. Robin barked so much that he had to go too. Mick had a big van with lots of things in the back. There were buckets and planks of wood and lots of plaster dust. It was very mucky. Charlie and Elly climbed up the steps to the front seat, and when they were up there they were so high they could see the roofs of cars. It was a terribly noisy van and all the things in the back rattled about, which scared poor Robin so much that he crouched on the floor all the way, and shivered.

When they got to the builders' yard it was absolutely enormous. The first thing they saw was a pile of enormous planks—and then another one, and another after that. There was a terrific whining noise, EEEEEOW EEEEEOW, that set their teeth on edge.

"That's them sawing the wood up into smaller pieces," said Mick. "We'll not go too near or they might take the tail off Mr Robin." Mick meant it as a joke but Robin put his ears back and hunched his shoulders. He didn't like the noise anyway.

They went to the side of the yard and watched a big crane picking up planks, swinging them round, and dropping them in different piles on the other side of the yard. The crane had a chain with a hook on it and a man tied the planks to the hook with rope.

They watched until something a bit scary happened: the crane went a bit faster than usual and the planks weren't tied on quite right, and when they started moving round they were spinning, and they spun so fast they hit the fence, BANG! Robin and Charlie and Elly nearly jumped out of their skins. The crane men shouted for a minute but there was nothing broken so they just carried on. Mick said, "We'd better go and get the sand," and they went into the builders' yard shop to find someone to serve them.

When they got inside, they had to stand around for a while looking at shelves and shelves of shiny nails and bolts and screws and hammers and taps and screwdrivers and everything you could think of that a builder might need. The men behind the counter kept rushing backwards and forwards with bits of paper, muttering to themselves and getting things off the shelves and making little piles of tools and things on the counter.

They were so busy they hardly even looked up, but sometimes they did, and then they would speak to the person they were serving and it wouldn't make any sense at all.

"I'll take three lengths of downpipe and three of gutter and ten gutter clips and six downpipe clips, and a shoe," said a tall man in overalls.

"Why does he want a shoe?" Charlie wondered.

"Same reason I want me boots polished, sure he wants to be a film star like meself," said Mick. "Some hope he's got."

This was no help at all, and the man was still saying things you couldn't understand, like three one hundred and ten downpipe bends and a stop-end outlet and four rodding eyes, when Sailor came in. That was exciting but he hadn't got time to talk to them much, apart from saying hello. And when Sailor started to talk to one of the men behind the counter, even he was talking nonsense!

"Six lengths of four by two width by four metres," said Sailor.

"Sawn, or P.A.R.?" said the man.

"P.A.R.," said Sailor.

Charlie and Elly were beginning to get bored, so it was good that Mick was served next. He asked for the sand and they went out again into the yard to get it.

CHARLIE AND ELLY STORIES

The man had lots of bags of sand, Mick took some of the bright yellow kind and they got back in the van again and went home. When they got there Mum had gone out. There was a note on the kitchen table which simply said Back Soon.

"Sure, it's too late to do anything much more today," said Mick, "I'll just be getting up me tower for a look to see if it's all right for the night." He meant his scaffolding tower that he had for climbing up to the roof. Mick went out and he put his stuck-on boots onto the first rung of the tower and he began to climb. He got higher and higher. He went more slowly than he usually did, mostly he almost jumped up in one go. But this time, when he got nearly all the way to the top his foot slipped and his hand slipped, and he crashed all the way down to the ground and lay there.

Charlie and Elly were indoors and so for a while nobody knew about it, but soon Robin came down from the end of the garden and he saw Mick lying on the ground, moaning a little, and he went inside at once to fetch the children. He trotted up to them and began to cry very loudly and then he ran to the door and back again.

"Robin's talking," said Charlie.

"What is it, Robin?" said Elly.

Robin cried even louder and ran back to the door, whirring his tail round and round like a helicopter.

"He says to go in the garden," said Charlie. So they did. Mick had woken up properly and was leaning on one elbow.

66

"I should have taken me boots off before they got full of concrete," he said.

"What's wrong?" said Elly.

"I think I've twisted me ankle," said Mick. "In fact I'm sure I have. It feels like a corkscrew. I don't know why there aren't holes in the ground where it went in."

Charlie and Elly were upset and a bit frightened. "Mum, Mum!" they shouted.

"I'll be all right in a minute or two," said Mick, "and your mum'll probably be back." But after what seemed like ages and ages Mum still wasn't back, and Mick decided to try and stand up. He sat up first and then he put his good foot down and pushed himself up with his hand. Then he stood on his hurt foot as well —and fell down again shouting "ow ow ow ow!"

Charlie and Elly whispered together. "We'd better get Mr Patel," they said. Charlie was very excited.

"Mr Patel could help," said Elly to Mick, and the children set off to find him.

It was quite an adventure. Mum let them go to the shop sometimes, but that was when she was in the house. They went to the front door, and were clever enough to wedge it open with a stool. They hadn't got a key so they had to make sure they could get back in. Then they went out of the door and down the street. Mr Patel's corner shop was only a few houses down and it was on the same side of the street. They ran as fast as they could, and burst into the shop, puffing and panting.

"Mick's hurt himself, please come, he's fallen over," Charlie gasped.

"What is it, Charlie?" said Mr Patel. "Mick the builder? Is he badly hurt?"

"He can't walk," said Charlie.

Mr Patel put a notice in the shop door saying Back in Five Mins, and hurried to Charlie and Elly's house and out into the garden.

"I think I've twisted me ankle, at least, I hope it isn't broken altogether." Mick tried to smile but it wasn't a very big smile.

"Don't worry, Mick, I'll have a look at it," said Mr Patel. He rolled Mick's trouser up and took off his boot. The boot came off quite easily, whatever Mick had said about it being stuck on. He felt gently around Mick's ankle and for once Mick hadn't got a joke ready. He made a lot of faces though, and once or twice he said "ouch!"

"It's only a sprain, nothing broken," said Mr Patel, "I'll bandage it very tight for you and you'll be all right in a couple of days."

"Sure, that's good news," said Mick, "I don't have to lose me leg then?"

"No."

"How can you be so sure?" said Mick, who seemed to be getting back to his old cheeky self again.

"I have done more than one course in First Aid," said Mr Patel, rather seriously.

Mum came home then, and there was lots and lots to tell her, but first about Mick's ankle.

"Poor Mick," she said, "let's all have some tea outside, and then you can tell me everything."

So she made some tea and took it out, and everybody had some.

"Charlie and Elly are very clever," said Mick, "and Mr Patel, now he's a genius."

"I want to be a builder when I grow up," said Elly.

"So do I," said Charlie.

"Just make sure you don't go falling off the scaffolding in your concrete boots," said Mick.

Charlie and Elly's Shop

One day Charlie and Elly were feeling bored, so they went and asked their mum what to do. Mum was in her work room doing some drawings for a magazine, but she stopped and said, "What about a bit of fruit-picking? The beans and pears and apples are ready." It sounded like good fun.

"Come on Robin!" they shouted, and they all ran off down the garden. It was the end of the summer so the flowers and trees were looking gorgeous, and it was a nice warm day, just the sort of day to be out.

Charlie was four and Elly was five, and Charlie was not as tall as Elly, so he picked beans. Elly picked fruit, though she had to climb on a chair to reach. Mum brought the chair out, and then Elly moved it round the trees. Sometimes Elly couldn't get the apples and pears, even with the chair, and then Charlie would climb up the trees and shake the branches out for her. Charlie was brilliant at climbing trees, just like a monkey, Mum said.

But when Charlie raced up a tree, Robin got very cross. He stood at the foot of the tree and barked and barked, and jumped up. It made him mad that he couldn't get up himself.

"Shut up, Robin!" Charlie said.

"Dogs can't climb trees!" said Elly.

But he still did it, jumping up and making a fuss. So it *was* good fun for a while, but then they got fed up with picking.

"Hmmm," said Charlie. Elly thought of the answer.

"I know what, let's go and say hello to Miss Myrtle," she said. They went up to the fence between the gardens, and as they got there the old lady saw them and shouted, "Hello, Charlie and Elly!"

"We've been picking things," they said, "but now we don't know what to do."

"Come with me to Mr Patel's while we all think of something," said Miss Myrtle. "I've got to get my newspaper."

Charlie and Elly went through the gap in the fence and the three of them walked down to the corner shop. Inside, Jackson and Mrs Rotten were having a loud argument about something. They were both shouting. Poor Mr Patel was just standing back. He hated rows, especially in his shop.

"No he didn't, leave it out, Mrs. He didn't and that's it!" Jackson yelled.

"Don't lie to me, it must have been him," shouted Mrs Rotten. "And you let him out deliberately!"

"I never, I can't stop him going out, he's a cat, isn't he? You're always on at me for nothing."

"Whatever's the matter?" said Miss Myrtle.

Jackson and Mrs Rotten both started shouting at once.

"He lets it do anything!"—"She can't leave me alone!"—"He's a juvenile delinquent!"

It turned out that Mrs Rotten was saying Jackson's cat had stolen a pork chop from her kitchen table, even though she hadn't actually seen him do it.

"Can't have been my cat!" Jackson suddenly shouted triumphantly.

"What do you mean it can't?" shouted Mrs Rotten.

"He's a vegetarian!" yelled Jackson, laughing.

Miss Myrtle said, "This is awfully silly, you two. *Awfully* silly. Stop arguing while I'm in the shop. You can carry on afterwards."

72

They did shut up for the few moments it took for Miss Myrtle to buy her newspaper, but as soon as she and Charlie and Elly were out of the shop they could hear them starting again.

"Poor Mr Patel, what a noise," said Miss Myrtle. "It must be difficult keeping a shop . . ." She stopped and thought for a minute. "We could play shops in your play house, and sell the beans and things you've picked."

Charlie and Elly thought that was a brilliant idea, so they all went back to the play house. They put the beans and fruit on the table in piles, and then they were ready to open. Elly was shopkeeper first and stood behind the table, while Miss Myrtle sat on the bench. Charlie came in the door and said, "I want some apples."

"Yes sir," said Elly, "how many?"

"Three," said Charlie.

"Here you are, sir," said Elly. "Fifty pence."

Charlie reached in his pocket and pretended to get the money. Then he handed over a pretend fifty pence.

"I want paying properly," said Elly.

"That's not fair, you know I haven't got any," said Charlie, getting cross.

Miss Myrtle said, "Why don't you use leaves for money? I'll get you some." She hurried off and soon came back with the leaves.

"There you are, Elly," said Charlie, still a bit cross. He gave some leaves and took the apples and left the shop.

Miss Myrtle came in next. She decided to play a trick.

"I'd like a bag of sweets, please," she said. Elly thought, Miss Myrtle's teasing me. She knows we haven't got sweets.

"There you are," Elly said, handing over the biggest apple she could find. "That's the best bag of sweets. It costs fifty pence."

"Oh, but I wanted a bigger bag than that," Miss Myrtle said, just to be difficult.

"You could have two bags," said Elly.

"Oh all right," said Miss Myrtle, and she took the two big apples and gave Elly lots and lots of leaves. She went out of the shop, but then she came straight back in again.

"Let's play being different people doing their shopping," she said.

"Who?" said Elly.

"I'm the king!" announced Charlie, who was always imagining things. "I want things for my rocket!"

"Kings don't have rockets," said Elly, practical as always.

"What do you want for your rocket, sire?" asked Miss Myrtle politely.

"Guns!" said Charlie loudly.

"I'm afraid we're fresh out of guns, sire," said Miss Myrtle, who hated things like that. "Let's be real people who we know," she said quickly. "I'll be Mrs Rotten."

So for a while they played at being some of the people

in the street: cross Mrs Rotten, cheeky Jackson, quiet Sailor. Then Miss Myrtle said she was going to be someone they knew very well, but they'd got to guess who. She came bustling into the shop and said: "I'm terribly sorry, hang on a sec, I've lost my list for a minute," and she was puffing a bit and pretending to look through all her pockets and her bag. "Hold on, sorry, don't serve anybody else, pound of onions and then I'll find it," she said, rummaging a bit more.

"It's Mum!" squealed Elly, "she always says that!"

"What do I always say?" asked Mum, who had arrived at the door of the play house just in time to hear Elly squealing.

"Lost your list," said Elly.

"We're playing shops," explained Miss Myrtle, "I was being you. Sorry," she finished, but she was giggling almost as much as the children. Mum wasn't really cross though.

"I think you should carry on until you get to the bit where I lose my purse," she said.

"You do it, Mum," said Elly.

"All right, pretend I've just bought these beans," said Mum. "Oh crikey, I can't find my purse!" she squeaked, "I had it a minute ago in the baker's shop. Hang on!"

Mum felt in her pockets, and looked all round the play house—on its floor and out of its windows and through its door, and even on its ceiling. All the time, she got more and more frantic.

"Got it!" she suddenly cried. "It was in my bag all the time."

Mum found her pretend purse in her pretend bag, pretended to pay for some beans and left the shop.

Then Robin came in. He'd got fed up with playing shops and had gone off down to the trees, but now he came back. He rather hoped the game would be over, but Miss Myrtle kept it going.

"Here's another customer," she said, patting Robin's head. Robin put his front paws up on the table.

"Can I help you?" said Elly politely.

Robin quite liked apples, so he was sniffing at them and wagging his tail.

"Say please, Robin, give me your paw," said Elly.

Robin was already reaching forward to grab an apple in his mouth, and he tried to give a paw at the same time, and somehow he managed to knock the whole table over, so all the apples and pears and beans and leaves fell down and rolled around the floor.

"Oh *Robin!*" said Charlie and Elly and Miss Myrtle together. But Robin didn't mind, he just ran off to the trees and they ran after him. By the time they caught up, they weren't cross any more. It seemed just as much fun to play tig, after all.

Miss Myrtle and the Tram

Charlie and Elly played a lot in the play house Dad and Sailor had built for them, and the game they liked best for most of that summer was shops. They were playing it one morning when Miss Myrtle came in, but she didn't look at all well.

"Hello, Charlie and Elly," she said, "I'll just sit down for a minute."

Miss Myrtle was very old, much older than you'd think for somebody so jolly. Sometimes she played hopscotch or hide-and-seek with Charlie and Elly, but at other times she didn't feel so bright, and she got dizzy and tired. Charlie and Elly offered to get her a glass of water.

"No thanks," said the old lady, "I'll be all right. It's all that gardening, straight after going to the shops . . . It was much easier when the tram used to bring me home," she said.

Charlie and Elly knew what a tram was because Miss Myrtle had told them before. It was a sort of bus that ran on rails, like a train, but the rails were in the road. Miss Myrtle could even remember the ones that didn't have engines but got pulled along by a horse.

"Did I ever tell you about the time the horse ran away?" Miss Myrtle said now.

"Tell us *again!*" said Charlie and Elly together. It was one of their favourite stories.

"Well." Miss Myrtle spoke and paused as if to get up steam for talking. "It was a day just like today, all warm and bright, a lovely day. The tram was nearly full up and everybody was feeling happy because it was so nice. All the same it was a weekday, so the people were on their way to business in the shops and offices and everything. Well, at the bottom of Rathbone Hill the tram stopped to take on an extra horse. Two horses pulled it usually, but then they would put another one on to make three."

"Why?" asked Charlie, who knew perfectly well really but just wanted to hear it all again.

"Because you know Rathbone Hill, it's very, very steep and two horses couldn't put that big heavy tram up with all the people in it, so they used to bring another horse and harness it up too."

"Oh, I get it," said Charlie.

"Good," said Miss Myrtle. She stopped for a minute.

"Go on," said Elly.

"Yes. What happened was, they brought the extra horse up and they were fiddling with the harness of the others, and the new horse was very frisky that day and it got loose. Something must have startled it because it shied away and began to run up the hill towards the park. Everybody was scared at first, they were screaming and shouting, but somehow the horse got up the street without causing an accident, which was very lucky indeed. The horse went straight for the fields around Mervyn Hall, you know, the big house where the park is now, and everybody got off the tram. A good many of the passengers went running after the horse. I did!" said Miss Myrtle proudly.

"What happened then?" asked the children.

"That was when it got very funny," answered Miss Myrtle, "because there were so many· people chasing this wretched horse. We could *not* catch it but we very soon didn't care, because it was such a lovely day and we weren't at work. It was the sort of day for a picnic or an outing to the seaside—like on a bank holiday, you know. While we were running around after the wretched horse, I think half the businesses in the village couldn't open at all! I certainly saw the three tailors who worked in the little shop in Church Street. Everybody from the tailors' shop was there: Tommy, Terry, and Wilfred. Nobody can have got measured for a suit *that* morning . . ."

Miss Myrtle was getting into a world of her own. She was looking out of the window as though she couldn't see anything. She broke off the story and started humming to herself, with a funny little smile on her face.

Charlie got very impatient.

"Go on, then what?" he almost shouted, even though he knew. But Miss Myrtle began to tell them a bit of the story they'd never heard before.

"We got the horse into a corner of the field and we had it trapped; we were in a ring round it and closing it in. So we got closer and closer. All of a sudden it bolted through the ring and we all fell over on top of each other. It was funny in a way." Miss Myrtle stopped for a moment. "But I fell against Wilfred, one of the tailors, and he said, 'Well my luck's in today and no mistake', which was very forward of him, I thought. So I said, 'Don't you be so sure of yourself'. But he was a one, that Wilfred, he was brighter than the others and he did used to make me laugh! Used to wink and make jokes, but not too saucy like the others. We used to laugh at such silly things! So when I fell on him and he said 'Let's walk to the river', I went along. I thought it wouldn't matter for five minutes but we got talking and laughing and, before you knew it, we'd forgotten the time. We started playing a game where you throw sticks in the river and see which comes out first."

Charlie and Elly sometimes threw sticks themselves, so they knew about that too.

"Wilfred did nearly all the actual making in the tailors' shop," Miss Myrtle went on, changing the subject a bit. "Tommy was the cutter and Terry saw to the customers."

"Did they really make things in the shop?" Elly wondered.

"Oh yes," said Miss Myrtle, "and very funny they looked too. Sometimes the three of them would sit cross-legged on the long mahogany counter like a row of elves, stitching and gossiping: when a customer came in they'd have been sitting like that for so long, their legs were stuck with cramp and they'd tumble off the counter one after another with their legs still crossed!" Miss Myrtle laughed quite a lot about this, and Elly laughed a bit.

"Let's play shops some more," said Charlie, who was getting a bit bored, but Elly still had some questions.

"Was Wilfred your boyfriend?" she asked.

"Never you mind, Miss Nosy Elly," said Miss Myrtle, not cross, but meaning it all the same.

"Why didn't you get married?" Elly persisted.

"I wasn't cut out for it," said Miss Myrtle.

"What's that mean?" said Charlie.

"It means I'll finish my story," said Miss Myrtle quickly. "Because Wilfred and I were playing around for so much longer than we meant, we forgot completely that we were supposed to be at work. Then it got very late. By the time we got back to the field the horse had gone and all the people had gone as well, so we had to hurry back to work ourselves. We walked back to Rathbone Hill and caught another Number Three tram, and there we were."

"Is that the end?" asked Elly.

"Well, not quite," said Miss Myrtle, "because we were very late back. Everyone else had gone back to

business but us, and we got a dreadful ticking-off from our bosses. Quite dreadful! In those days you weren't even ten minutes late for work in the morning, so you can imagine our knuckles were rapped."

"What with?" Charlie wanted to know.

"Not *really*, Charlie, it just means we were in trouble. But we'd had a lovely day," said Miss Myrtle. Then she stood up. The story was finished and she was back in the shop again.

"I'll take six beans," she said to Charlie, "how much is that?"

"Two leaves," said Charlie, very business-like.

"Shall I wrap them up for you, madam?" asked Elly.

"Yes, please," said Miss Myrtle.

So Charlie counted out the beans while Miss Myrtle went to pick two leaves, and Elly put the beans in a bag. Miss Myrtle came back in and paid for the beans and took the bag and left the shop.

"Thank you very much, see you again soon," she said as she was going.

"Thank you, Miss Myrtle," said Elly.

"Don't go!" said Charlie, "play with us!"

So Miss Myrtle came back into the shop pretending to be somebody else, and they played shops all the rest of the morning.

Charlie and Amina

In September Elly got ready to go to school. Now that she was five it was time to start, and she was looking forward to it very much. She and Mum had talked about it a bit all through the summer and Charlie felt a bit left out. He wasn't going to go, because he was only four. But however left out he'd felt with them talking about it was nothing to how he felt when the first day of term came and they actually went.

A terrific fuss was made of her, everybody got up specially early and she had a new bag to put things in. Charlie wouldn't put his clothes on.

"Not going," he kept saying.

"Come on, Charlie, for heaven's sake, don't make us late," Mum said. But he sat on the floor and wouldn't move.

"I'll take you to the park and we can find George," said Mum, "just you and me and Robin. What about that?"

Charlie put his socks on, sulkily.

So then, every day Elly would be coming home full of stories of what had happened, and sometimes she was brought home by her new schoolfriends' parents, and her friends would come and they'd all chatter and play together. Elly still played with Charlie a bit, but not all that much, and he was left to himself for most of the days.

Somehow it was very different when you were really on your own. Charlie had always done things by himself, when Elly was around, like acrobatics and climbing things, and he didn't talk as much as she did —Elly was more of a bustling sort of person, making things, and bossing everybody. But it's very different doing something by yourself with somebody else there, from how it is doing something on your own with nobody about at all. Nobody except Mum, that is, but she was usually busy anyway.

One day, about two or three weeks after the beginning of Elly's school term, Mum took Charlie and Robin to the park again. They wandered around in the sunshine doing all the usual things: feeding the ducks, going on the swings, chasing Robin and throwing sticks. After a while they saw Mrs Rotten.

"Quick, Charlie, hide behind the big tree!" said Mum, laughing a bit because it was too late anyway; they'd been seen and Mrs Rotten was coming towards them.

"Good morning," said Mrs Rotten, smiling her stuck-on smile. She was clearly in one of her better moods, when she wasn't all that bad, but her smile always looked unreal. "Hello, Charlie, all on your own, do you want an ice cream?" she said. "We could have a cup of tea if you fancy it," she said to Mum.

They all walked slowly towards the big house in the middle of the park.

"I expect you're missing your sister, now she's at school," said Mrs Rotten. When she wasn't in one of her awful bad tempers and screeching at people like Jackson, even Mrs Rotten sometimes understood things.

"Playing with Robin," said Charlie, looking gloomy.

They got to the big house and Charlie and Robin got a choc-ice each, but then Mum and Mrs Rotten started talking, so that was boring.

Charlie stared round the room in the big house. The house was in the middle of the park, and one of the downstairs rooms was used as a sort of café all through the summer. But it still looked quite like it looked when it was lived in. It had a big old fireplace you could stand up in, if you were Charlie's height. Round the grate was a big brass fence thing, to stop the fire falling out into the room, Mum said. Charlie played at being a lion behind the brass fence, and growled fiercely at everybody, but nobody took any notice.

Charlie wandered around and Mum and Mrs Rotten talked and talked, and then Charlie saw that Robin wasn't there any more. The door to the big house was wide open because it was such a nice day. He had just wandered off.

"Robin's gone!" said Charlie to Mum.

"Oh Charlie, go and look for him then, will you? But don't go further than the ponds," said Mum. "See if you can find George to help you."

Charlie was halfway through the door already, it was so much nicer out.

"Robin! Robin!" he yelled, running off through the playground. Some children were playing on the swings and they stared at him.

"Lost your mum?" said one of their mums.

"No," said Charlie. "Robin."

"Who's Robin?" she asked.

"His dog," said George the parky, appearing at that moment. "Don't worry, Charlie, he won't have gone far. I'm going down to the ponds now, I'll take you if you like."

So George and Charlie set off together, past the bowling green and the tennis courts.

"Robin!" shouted Charlie.

"He won't be there," said George.

"How d'you know?" said Charlie.

"Dogs never play tennis," said George.

"Robin does," said Charlie.

"Oh no he doesn't!" said George.

"Oh yes he does," said Charlie. This was one of their favourite silly conversations and they went on with it for ages, past the putting green and the adventure playground and the paddling pool, but there was still no sign of Robin.

Eventually they got down to the ponds but they *still* hadn't found Robin, and this was very odd because

Robin usually came when he was called, and anyway, the park was quite small to get lost in. They went to the far side of the ponds, and there was Amina with her gran. Amina was Mr Patel's little girl.

"Hello," said Charlie.

"Hello," said Amina.

"Do you want to play?" said Charlie, forgetting Robin instantly.

"All right," said Amina.

Charlie had only ever seen Amina in the shop, so he didn't know her much really. They ran off to the trees, with George and Amina's gran watching.

First they played hide-and-seek, and George played too. Amina's gran just went on watching. She was a very quiet old lady and she didn't speak much English. George was good at finding the children, but terrible at hiding. He always left his big boots sticking out from behind the trees where he was, or somehow his cap fell off into the path just where you could see. Amina was quite good, but very timid. Charlie was the best of all. He was always brilliant at doing things out of doors, or anything where you had to run or climb.

"Let's climb the trees!" he said suddenly.

"You're joking aren't you, Charlie?" said George.

Charlie could go up trees faster than almost anybody and he set off at great speed, but Amina's gran shook her head and called Amina.

"Come down and play something else," George said rather firmly. "What about hopscotch, like you play with Miss Myrtle?"

They found a sharp bit of stone and scratched hopscotch squares on the path. George wasn't supposed to let anybody do that, much less help them, but Charlie and Elly had been special favourites of his ever since the adventure when Jackson fell through the ice. Even so, he thought it was time for him to go; he had work to do, after all. "See you later," said George.

By this time everyone had forgotten Robin altogether. They went on forgetting him, and Charlie and Amina played hopscotch for what seemed like ages until Amina's gran told Amina they had to go.

"Play tomorrow?" said Charlie to Amina. She looked happy and nodded.

Charlie, Amina and Amina's gran went back to the big house in the middle of the park, and Charlie was in a very different mood from the one in which he'd left it. Mum and Mrs Rotten were standing on the steps, shading their eyes from the sun and staring into the park for Charlie. Robin was standing beside them.

"Wherever have you been, Charlie?" said Mum, "Robin came back hours ago."

"Playing with Amina," said Charlie. Amina and her gran just smiled.

"That's good," said Mum, "did you have a good time? You must have done, judging by how long you've been. What did you play?"

"Hopscotch," explained Charlie briefly.

"Perhaps Amina would like to come and play with you tomorrow, in our garden?" suggested Mum.

"YES!" yelled Charlie.

"Would you like that, Amina?" asked Mum.

And Amina, who was very shy, just nodded, but her face was smiling very much.

"Is that all right?" said Mum to Amina's gran.

Amina's gran nodded and smiled too.

After that, sometimes when Elly came home and Charlie and Amina were still playing, they hardly even had time to say hello.

Charlie and Elly
and Royce

Mum and Dad and Charlie and Elly were having breakfast one autumn morning when they heard Miss Myrtle's doorbell ring.

"Good heavens," said Mum.

"Good heavens, what?" said Dad.

"Good heavens, they've really got here; Miss Myrtle's niece from America with her little boy," said Mum.

"Oh," said Dad. He wasn't all that interested, but Charlie and Elly wanted to know lots more, especially about the little boy.

"What's he called?"—"How old is he?"—"What's he like?" they asked.

Mum said the Americans were called Froehlich— funny name, said the children—and that the boy was called Royce.

"And he only eats Rolls," Dad put in.

"What d'you mean?" said Charlie.

"It's a joke, Rolls Royce," said Mum, "only it isn't funny. Stop interrupting," she said crossly to Dad. Mum said that Royce was seven, which was even older than Elly. Mum couldn't tell them very much because she had never met these American visitors, but she thought Royce had never been to England before.

This didn't stop the questions, though.

"What's he look like?"

"I *don't know*," said Mum.

"Americans have green ears," said Dad suddenly, "and television aerials on their heads."

"WHAT!" squeaked Charlie.

"It's a joke, stupid," said Elly.

With or without green ears the children were dying to meet Royce. They went outside and crept right up to the gate between the gardens, and waited for what seemed like ages and ages. They could hear voices, but not what was being said. At last Miss Myrtle called them and they ran through.

"This is my niece Mrs Froehlich and this is Royce. And these are Charlie and Elly and Robin," said Miss Myrtle.

The Americans looked fairly ordinary really; Mrs Froehlich was tall and seemed nice and Royce had dark hair and a red T-shirt with writing on it. Everybody said hello except Charlie, who was trying to look round the side of Royce's head.

"Not green," Charlie said, in a very cheated sort of voice.

"What isn't green?" asked Miss Myrtle.

"His ears," said Charlie.

"Charlie, what *are* you talking about?" said Miss Myrtle. "Go and play in the garden all of you while I talk to Mrs Froehlich."

So the three children and Robin set off through Miss Myrtle's garden to go to Charlie and Elly's.

"Is Robin your dog?" said Royce, to start the conversation.

"Yes," said Elly, and Robin barked very loud, WOOF WOOF, in his deepest voice.

"Say hello to Robin," said Elly.

"OK, hello Robin, how ya doing, you're looking good," said Royce in a friendly way. Then he stopped for a moment. "Hey, this is weird, talking with a dog!" he said. "We don't talk with dogs in New York. We don't *have* dogs in New York."

"No dogs?" said Charlie, horrified. He couldn't think what a place might be like without dogs.

"What *do* you have in New York?" they asked, as they all walked back through the gate into the children's garden.

"I don't know. We got different things. It's different, I guess. Looks different. Big buildings," said Royce.

"What games do you play?" Elly wanted to know.

"Round about Hallowe'en we do trick-or-treat," Royce said. "Hey, it's Hallowe'en this week, isn't it? We could do that now."

"What's Hallowe'en?" said Charlie.

"Oh *you* know, Charlie, when the witches come," said Elly, in a very superior way that she had sometimes when she knew things.

"What witches?" asked Charlie.

"I never heard about any witches," Royce agreed.

"Witches come and ride through the sky, and it's all

magic and you have to watch out," said Elly.

"What for?" asked Charlie.

"Oh nothing much, I don't think they do anything but they just might," said Elly. And as that was all she knew about it, they had to make do with it.

"We do trick-or-treat," repeated Royce.

"I know how to do that," said Elly, who seemed to know practically everything.

"I don't," said Charlie, rather gloomily. Some days he felt as though Elly was a bit much, and it looked as though this was going to be one of them. But then Royce began to explain.

"It's really terrific, you get all dressed up and you paint your face, and then you go round to the grown-ups and say, 'Trick-or-treat?' Or you say, 'Trick-or-treat, smell my feet, give me something good to eat'. If they're chicken they say 'Treat', and that's good because they have to give you something, sweets or money or something. But if they say 'Trick', it's even better, you get to play a trick on them."

"What like?" Charlie wanted to know.

"Oh, anything," said Royce. "The little kids just pull their hair or something, the bigger ones ask riddles and play jokes."

"Let's do jokes!" Charlie shrieked, "I want to do jokes!"

"Some of them aren't too nice, the tricks," said Royce, "like, one is to throw toilet paper out of the window and drag it all over the yard . . . We could soap the windows though."

"What?" said Charlie and Elly together. Robin growled a bit. He didn't like soap very much.

"You just draw something on their windows in soap."

"Let's do it to Miss Myrtle!" Charlie said. So they went off and found Miss Myrtle, who was talking to Royce's mother.

"Trick-or-treat, Miss Myrtle!"

"Trick-or-treat?" said Miss Myrtle. "Treat, I suppose. Go and get something out of my sweetie jar."

So they did, but Charlie was dying to do a trick so he ran back and said, "Say trick, say trick, go on."

"Oh children, we're talking. All right then, trick, but don't make it too horrible."

Charlie shouted "TRICK TRICK TRICK" and did a sort of war dance, before rushing off to the bathroom for some soap. He came downstairs again and drew a face on Miss Myrtle's window.

"Oh *Charlie*," said Miss Myrtle. But then she looked at it for a minute and said, "That is a good face, though."

"You're supposed to write something," Royce said.

"Can't," said Charlie.

"That's OK, I will," said Royce, and he put TRICK-OR-TREAT CHARLIE THE TURKEY beside the picture.

"What's it say?" said Charlie.

"It says, 'Trick-or-treat, Charlie the turkey'," said Miss Myrtle, "but what does it mean? Why is Charlie a turkey?"

"A turkey's a crazy guy, really off the wall," said Royce. "I like Charlie so I wrote that. Charlie's a great guy. He's out to lunch. Green ears!" he finished, laughing.

"Dad said green." Charlie tried to explain, but he only managed to sound crazier.

"Don't worry, Charlie," said Miss Myrtle, "that's a wonderful face you've drawn." Actually Miss Myrtle wasn't very keen on the window soaping, but she wanted to cheer Charlie up.

"I'm drawing Robin," announced Elly, and she did. Her picture was quite good, but not as good as

Charlie's. Then Miss Myrtle couldn't resist joining in, and she did a magnificent picture of a turkey with lots of feathers—a very peculiar turkey, because instead of a turkey's head with a beak and a comb, it had Charlie's head and Charlie's dreamy little face that always looked as though Charlie was somewhere else.

Everybody thought it was a wonderful picture, and everybody wanted to draw something. Elly fetched extra soap and they decided to do one big picture with each of them drawing a person or an animal, all round the pictures they'd already drawn. Before long the window was covered in drawings and it looked as though Robin the dog was chasing Charlie the turkey into the arms of Miss Myrtle, who was being propped up from behind by a very small Martian with aerials twanging out from all over his head.

Royce's mum was quite an artist. She drew little animals and stars and moons all round the edges of the window. When the window was almost covered she drew a joke: she put a river behind the picture of Royce the Martian, and the river was so close to him it looked as though he would fall into it any minute, *splosh!*

"Now that the window's covered, you'd better show Royce an English game," said Miss Myrtle. There was silence for a whole minute while they couldn't think of one.

WOOF WOOF WOOF WOOF WOOF WOOF WOOF WOOF said Robin.

"Playing with Robin!" said Elly. "That's our best game, playing with Robin! Let's play tig!"

So they did!

Charlie and Elly's Bonfire Night

At the end of October, George the parky started to build an enormous bonfire in the park for Bonfire Night. He did one every year, and every year the same people would come and help him. Mick the builder was nearly always the first to offer help. He would bring huge lumps of wood from wherever he was working— wood that was too rough or rotten to be used in the houses. Sailor, who often worked as a carpenter, was just as good at bringing bits of wood and helping to build. George brought tree branches that he had picked up off the ground. Other people brought things from home, like big wooden boxes. Together, they all made an excellent fire. Mick and George and Sailor—and sometimes Jackson—built it up very well.

Charlie and Elly and Robin got very excited about all the preparations, and they went round to see what everyone was doing. Miss Myrtle and Mum were in charge of making baked potatoes and sausages for everybody on Bonfire Night, and they were wondering whether they'd ordered enough food to go round.

"What if that terrible Jackson gets there first and scoffs the lot?" Mum said.

"I should worry more about Sailor and Mick, if I were you," said Miss Myrtle.

"I'll shoot them all!" said Mum.

"Wait till the bonfire's built before you do that," said Miss Myrtle.

Charlie and Elly and Robin and Miss Myrtle went round to see Mr Patel. He was supplying all the fireworks, and Sailor was helping him to plan the display. It was to look very beautiful but both of them were very keen that no one should get hurt, so they were working out firework shows, one after another, and then changing them again.

"Too many rockets," said Mr Patel.

"Too near the people, if they go off sideways," said Sailor. But it didn't take them all that long, they'd had a lot of practice in years before.

"It will be excellent!" said Mr Patel at last.

"Don't do bangers!" said Elly.

"No bangers at all," said Sailor, "except the ones you eat."

"If there's any left," said Elly.

"What do you mean by that, Elly?" asked Mr Patel.

"Oh, nothing," said Elly.

"The fireworks will be superb," said Sailor, "we're going to have lots of big splashes like flowers opening, you'll be able to see it for miles, I should think."

Charlie's little friend Amina was in the shop, but she wasn't looking excited like all the others, in fact, she was looking a bit miserable.

"Hello!" said Charlie, but the little girl didn't reply.

Mr Patel said something to her in Indian but she still looked miserable.

"Amina doesn't like the fireworks," he explained. "She finds them quite frightening, all the flashes and explosions and things."

"She could stay in with Robin," said practical Elly, "he gets frightened as well."

"She'll miss the fire!" Charlie shouted. He loved Bonfire Night.

"But if she doesn't like it . . ." said Miss Myrtle.

"That is a good idea, Elly," said Mr Patel. "Amina stays in the house with her granny when there are fireworks, but she might like to play with Robin."

"Good," said Elly. She liked things to be settled.

Sailor was getting his coat on to go to the park, and he offered to take Charlie and Elly with him. Miss Myrtle went back to her house while the others picked up Robin, and then they set off. Sailor started to tell them about building the bonfire.

"How big is it?" said Charlie.

"Nearly as big as your house," said Sailor.

"Will it get bigger and bigger?" Elly asked.

"It can't get all that much bigger or it'll fall over," said Sailor, "but a bit bigger, yes."

Sailor told them who'd been building the bonfire.

"Not Dad?" Charlie wondered.

"NO!" squealed Elly. "He'd make it fall over!"

"Actually, he nearly did make it fall over," said Sailor, "but he was trying to be helpful."

Dad had brought some rotten old cupboards out of

Charlie and Elly's cellar and had taken them to the park and tried to put them on the bonfire himself, without asking Mick or George. The bonfire was very specially built and heavy things had to be placed very carefully on it. Dad could never see how to do things like that. When Sailor and George and Mick had rebuilt the bonfire they suggested to Dad that he'd better not help any more.

"I could do the drinks," Dad offered, rather sadly.

"All right, thanks," said the others.

By the time all that had been explained, Charlie and Elly and Sailor were in the park and could see the big bonfire. It was quite near the big house where you got drinks and ice creams from, and it was enormous. As they got closer to the bonfire they could see it was made of planks and branches and boxes, with bits of cardboard, and lumpish things you couldn't make out. It was enormous, not just high but big all round. It took a long time to walk round it.

"Hello Charlie and Elly, hello Sailor," said George the parky, appearing from behind the bonfire.

WOOF, said Robin, crossly. He hated being left out.

"Hello, Robin. *Sorry*," said George.

"The fire's looking bigger," said Sailor, "I think it will be very good. We've just planned the fireworks, me and Mr Patel."

"And will you still be here?" said George.

"Yes," said Sailor, "at least until the end of the month, it looks like."

104

"Sailor going away?" said Charlie, looking upset.

"Yes," said Sailor, "but it's a good trip for me, I'm going all round the world, I've never done that before in one voyage. I'm going to see places I've never seen before . . . Bali and Singapore . . . Tasmania and the Persian Gulf . . ."

Charlie was not to be distracted. He hated it when Sailor went away.

"Going soon?" he wanted to know.

"Quite soon," said Sailor, "but I'll send you lots of postcards . . ."

Suddenly Jackson appeared from behind the bonfire.

"All right?" he said. That meant hello.

"Right," said Sailor.

"Want any help?" Jackson asked.

"Not here," said Sailor, "but you could go and help Mr Patel sort out the fireworks, if you want. He's going to do the display. He might need you to help him put up posts for Catherine wheels, and things."

"Couldn't somebody else go?" Jackson wondered, looking doubtful. Mr Patel and he had never got on all that well. Mr Patel didn't shout at Jackson like Mrs Rotten did, but he was nervous of Jackson's sticking-out hair and his weird clothes so he didn't talk to him much. Because of that, Jackson didn't go into Mr Patel's shop very often.

"No, Jackson, you go," Sailor said. Sometimes Sailor fixed things without people realizing. He thought it might be good if Jackson and Mr Patel worked together, they might become better friends.

"Take Charlie and Elly home while I get on with this fire," he said.

"All right," said Jackson, scowling. He collected the children and went off. George and Mick and Sailor still had lots to do. New stuff had arrived for the fire and needed to be carefully stacked on it, and they'd decided to make a little fence to keep people away from the fireworks, so they could look without getting too close.

Jackson dropped Charlie and Elly at their house, and went down to see Mr Patel. Charlie and Elly found Mum and Miss Myrtle in fits of laughter.

"It's mean to laugh so much," Mum said, spluttering and giggling.

"You *mean* it's *rotten* to laugh so much," said Miss Myrtle, and they laughed even more.

It turned out that Mrs Rotten had been making bonfire toffee, but it hadn't worked very well.

"Couldn't break it with a sledgehammer!" Miss Myrtle said. "I told her she should use it to mend the roof, it's probably waterproof as well!"

"Goodness, that was cheeky, what did she say to that?" said Mum.

"She can't say that much to me because I'm so old," said Miss Myrtle, laughing.

"That's what's so funny." And they went off into more fits of laughter than before. It was ages before Charlie and Elly could find out what had happened. Mrs Rotten's bonfire toffee had set very, very hard in the tins. It was so hard you couldn't break it up into bits to eat. Miss Myrtle had said it might be better used for building houses.

"Will we get real toffee on Bonfire Night?" asked Elly, going straight to the point.

"Yes," said Mum, "Mrs Rotten's going to make another lot tomorrow. She'll go on till she gets it right. We shouldn't be making fun of her, really."

"Rotten of us," agreed Miss Myrtle.

When Bonfire Night finally came, everybody from miles around went into the park. It was an enormous crowd, and everyone looked really excited. Lots of people brought their own sparklers. Mum and Dad took Robin round to Mr Patel's to be with Amina and her gran, and then they all set off together: Charlie, Elly, Miss Myrtle, Mum, Dad, and Mr Patel.

The fire was already lit when they got to the park, and burning well. It made the air very bright and warm. Even so, Mum had made Charlie and Elly put their coats and hats and boots and gloves and scarves on, because the autumn was getting colder.

"Where's Jackson?" Mum said. "I want him to keep an eye on you two while I go and do the food." Dad had gone straight to the drinks. He was doing hot Ribena for children, and hot red wine for grown-ups.

They looked all round for Jackson but couldn't see him at all.

"That's funny," said Mum, "he said he'd meet us here."

"Wotcher," said a familiar voice. They all looked round, but they couldn't see Jackson.

"Good evenin', Charles and Eleanor," said the same voice. "Not speakin' or what?"

As they looked, an extraordinary sight peered out of the darkness. It *was* Jackson. But his spiky hair was all brushed down, and he had on an ordinary jacket and jeans—he looked just ordinary. A bit boring, was what Elly thought.

"Good heavens!" said Mum. "It *is* you!"

"Seems like it," he said. "Don't wind me up. I've got a job, ain't I?"

"That's brilliant, Jackson, a Saturday job is it?" Mum asked.

"That's right, Saturdays at Mr Patel's, only he's made me tidy up that's all."

"You look funny!" said Charlie suddenly.

"Not half as funny as you!" said Jackson, poking him in the ribs and tickling him. It started a sort of pretend fight and they forgot to stare at Jackson any more.

Soon the fireworks started, and they were absolutely wonderful. There were huge starbursts like big magic flowers, all in different colours. There were rockets that dropped red and blue and green stars down, big stars that exploded into smaller ones. Some of the rockets made funny zooshy noises that Elly didn't like very much, even though they weren't bangers.

Charlie loved every second of it. He stared and stared. He particularly liked the Catherine wheels because they could make you dizzy if you moved your head round with them. Elly was watching, but she was also busy saying hello to people she knew: Mick and Sailor and George the parky.

She was wandering around being sociable, when all of a sudden she heard some angry-sounding voices which seemed to be coming from the other side of the bonfire. She went further round. Through the crowd she saw two boys who were shouting at each other. One was Jackson, the other was a bigger boy with red hair.

"Naff off!" Jackson yelled.

"Yah, Nancy, you gone soft, you have," shouted the other boy.

They began dancing round each other like boxers.

"Corkscrew!"

"Carrot-head!"

"That's enough!" shouted a third voice. It was George the parky.

"'E's calling me a corkscrew!" Jackson was still shouting, but a bit quieter.

"I don't want to know who's calling what," said George, "just knock it off, the pair of you. It's a party, for heaven's sake." He turned to the big boy. "You'd better go to the house for five minutes and cool off," he said.

"Ain't going," the big boy said, truculently.

"You can come with me while I check everything's all right there," said George. "Now!" George spoke this time in a voice that really meant it. The boy's carrot head dropped, and he followed George, kicking at stones along the way.

"'E said I look a wally with my 'air brushed down," said Jackson, who was still very upset.

"Well, you do," said a familiar voice. It was Sailor, who had been watching but had kept out of it.

"Oh, that's bloomin great, that is, from my mucker. Great," said Jackson.

"You always look a wally, all the time, anyway. No point spoiling Bonfire Night about it," said Sailor, blipping him on the head cheerfully. Jackson managed a sort of grin.

Elly agreed heartily with all this and spoke up at last. "Ooh look, rockets!" she squealed.

The fireworks were almost over and they were reaching some of Sailor and Mr Patel's best displays. More rockets and starbursts and flowers opened, and now firework fountains went off one after another. They were spectacular.

All of a sudden the fireworks were over, and Mum and Miss Myrtle were hurrying round with baked potatoes and sausages. Everybody was very glad of them because the night was getting colder. After that, it was time for Mrs Rotten's bonfire toffee. Mrs Rotten offered it to everybody with a nice smile—she could be quite nice sometimes. Then people began to drift off home.

Over by the big house, George the parky started to bang with a stick on a big metal tray. Charlie and Elly and their friends went to see what was going on.

"I just want to say three cheers for everybody who helped build the fire!!" shouted George, "Hip Hip!"

"HOORAY!" shouted everybody. They cheered the fire, then the fireworks, then the food and drink, then Sailor because he was going away, then Jackson for his new look—and it looked as though once they'd started, they'd go on to cheer practically the whole world. But Sailor finished it off very nicely.

"I shall miss you all, but I'll be back!" he shouted. "Now, let's give three cheers for my two smallest friends, Charlie and Elly! Hip Hip!"

"HOORAY, HOORAY, HOORAY!" shouted everybody.

And that was the end of the best Bonfire Night that anybody could remember.